Lynn Chambers trained as a prir
spending time as a full-time m(
specialize in working with children with special educational needs.
Beyond her role as a professional teacher, she has over 25 years'
experience of working with children in holiday clubs and Sunday
schools. Lynn was Diocesan Children's Officer for St David's
Diocese from 2001 to 2006. She was ordained in 2005, served her
curacy in Carmarthen and is now Priest-in-Charge of the parishes
of Brechfa with Abergorlech and Llanfihangel Rhos-y-corn in West
Wales. Lynn is joint author of *Play and Pray through Lent* and *Play and
Pray through Advent*, both published by *Barnabas*.

Important information

Photocopy permission

The right to photocopy material in *Creative Ideas for Quiet Corners* is granted for the pages that contain the photocopying clause: 'Reproduced with permission from *Creative Ideas for Quiet Corners* published by Barnabas 2008 (ISBN 978 1 84101 546 0)', so long as reproduction is for use by the original purchaser. The right to photocopy material is not granted for anyone other than the original purchaser without written permission from BRF.

The Copyright Licensing Agency (CLA)

If you are resident in the UK and you have a photocopying licence with the Copyright Licensing Agency (CLA), please check the terms of your licence. If your photocopying request falls within the terms of your licence, you may proceed without seeking further permission. If your request exceeds the terms of your CLA licence, please contact the CLA directly with your request. Copyright Licencing Agency, 90 Tottenham Court Road, London W1T 4LP. Telephone: 020 7631 5555; fax: 020 7631 5500; email: cla@cla.co.uk; website: www.cla.co.uk. The CLA will provide photocopying authorization and royalty fee information on behalf of BRF.
BRF is a Registered Charity (No. 233280)

Creative Ideas for
Quiet Corners

14 visual prayer ideas for quiet moments with children

Lynn Chambers

Text copyright © Lynn Chambers 2008
Illustrations copyright © Mary Hall 2008
The author asserts the moral right
to be identified as the author of this work

Published by
The Bible Reading Fellowship
15 The Chambers, Vineyard
Abingdon OX14 3FE
United Kingdom
Tel: +44 (0)1865 319700
Email: enquiries@brf.org.uk
Website: www.brf.org.uk

ISBN 978 1 84101 546 0
First published 2008
10 9 8 7 6 5 4 3 2 1 0

Acknowledgments
Unless otherwise stated, scripture quotations are taken from the Contemporary English Version
of the Bible published by HarperCollins Publishers, copyright © 1991, 1992, 1995 American
Bible Society.

A catalogue record for this book is available from the British Library

Printed in Singapore by Craft Print International Ltd

Preface

My interest in multisensory worship spaces began when I represented the Church in Wales at a children's ministry conference in Chicago some years ago. The main foyer had been converted into a 'discovery centre', available for use at all times of the day and night. At whatever time of day I passed by, there were always people sitting on the floor or on cushions. Adults and children alike were quietly reading, drawing, writing, touching and handling objects. Although the area was defined only by banners hanging from the ceiling and was open to view, the people inside seemed oblivious to all that was going on around them.

The choice of materials available was impressive and there seemed to be something there for everyone, regardless of age or ability. There were books for adults and children that explored the theme of the day, together with assorted Bibles and Bible stories for all ages. There were craft materials and suggestions of things to make and do linked with the day's theme. There were pictures to look at and objects to feel and hold. Dotted around among the activities were questions to prompt thought and opportunities to respond to God in prayer.

There was no pressure of time. Some individuals stayed in one place while others moved slowly from one activity to another. Occasionally people interacted, sharing something they were reading or had made. There was a quiet sense of excitement, almost wonder. The discovery centre seemed like an oasis of calm amid the busyness of the conference.

Since attending the conference in Chicago, I have developed the idea of multisensory worship space and created quiet corners in churches, conferences, quiet days and in Bible study groups for people of all ages.

LYNN CHAMBERS

To Mike
my husband and best friend

Acknowledgments

I am grateful to all my colleagues on the Church in Wales Provincial Children's Team and in the Consultative Group on Ministry among Children. They have given me the space and opportunities to experiment with creative ideas for quiet corners. Special thanks also go to Sue Doggett, Commissioning Editor for *Barnabas* books, for encouraging and supporting me in the writing of this book.

✥

Contents

✣

Foreword

Lynn Chambers and I met many years ago as representatives of our church denominations at the Consultative Group on Ministry among Children, a network of Churches Together in Britain and Ireland. We spent a coffee break chatting and getting to know each other. The impression of Lynn that I took away with me that day, and have kept with me ever since, was one of a person who held an inner peace of such depth that I can only hope to come near to it.

What Lynn has done in *Creative Ideas for Quiet Corners* is to recognize the stillness that she holds within herself and to share it with us while helping us to discover it within ourselves. In particular, she encourages us to help children to find that very special place in which they can encounter God.

This book is about stillness, listening and speaking with the heart, and discovering the joy of quiet times. It is about creativity and stories; it is about our own story. The activities in this book do not have pass or fail grades; they simply help us to be part of the story, to live the story. How wonderful it is, in the chapter 'The family of God' (page 52), to see a dark cloth placed before you cover it in stars, all of whom are known to you because you have chosen each star to represent your family and friends, whoever you might recognize those people to be. In God's eyes they are all stars too!

But the greatest joy of this book, for me, is the recognition that the stillness, the quietness, the God-given creativity that we discover, is in the very depths of each and every one of us and that, once found, it will always be accessible. In the words of the author, we will always have a 'place where we can simply "be"'.

Karen Bulley, Moderator of CGMC and Pilots Development Officer, URC

✤

Introduction

What is a quiet corner?

A quiet corner is a place of discovery. It is multisensory, offering opportunities to look, feel, smell, taste and touch as you are drawn into stillness and prayer. It is a place where you can learn more about yourself and understand more about God. It is a place of growth where your relationship with God can develop. It is a place of worship, a quiet corner for prayer, a sacred space.

The beauty of a quiet corner is that it is non-directive. There are suggestions for use, but there is no pressure to use the materials in a prescribed way. Where there are several prayer areas or stations, it can be interesting to observe connections being made—for example, a cross on the world map, confetti stars floating on the water in the pebble pool, or a model of a sheep at the foot of a cross. The non-directive approach is not without its difficulties. For some people the process is too open-ended. There is often no visible end product and results are not easily measured. Our society is geared to results and accountability. From a very young age our children are pressured to achieve and their levels of attainment are compared with others of the same age, not just locally but nationally.

Where children are concerned—and even for many adults— a quiet corner may be a rare place where they can simply 'be'. Individuals can choose how to spend their time in a peaceful environment by reading, doing or simply sitting quietly. The quiet area is aimed at helping them learn about God and enter into a relationship with God in a non-pressured way, at their own pace and on their own terms. The overall results can only be gauged over time. It is to be hoped that by spending time with God, listening as well as talking, the fruit of the Holy Spirit will become more evident in adults and children alike, so that all will develop love, happiness, peace, patience, kindness, goodness, faithfulness, gentleness and self-control (Galatians 5:22–23).

Why do we need a quiet corner?

We live in an increasingly busy and demanding world. Nearly everywhere we go, we are bombarded by noise—in shops, on the street, when we travel. When we do encounter silence, we often find it threatening or disturbing and we try to fill the silence with noise. How many of us automatically switch on the radio or television as soon as we get home or when we are driving alone in the car?

In our attempts to involve young people in the life of the church, it is often assumed that young people like noise, movement and busyness. This is reflected in lively youth groups, and family or all-age worship with lots of activity and movement. In many of our churches, music fills the silences before and after services and during the administration of Holy Communion. Music and lively activity can certainly enhance worship but it is also possibly to overlook the benefits of quietness. When God met Elijah, he did not speak through the strong wind, the earthquake or the fire but in the gentle breeze (1 Kings 19:1–13).

Close your eyes for a moment and listen. What can you hear? If you live in the city, you may well hear traffic noise, sirens, roadworks, music from passing vehicles or open windows, mobile phone ringtones, the voices of passers-by or children in the school playground or park along the road. If you live in a rural area you might hear aircraft noise, tractors, chainsaws, birdsong and animal sounds. If you are at home there may also be the sounds from the television or radio, the rumble of the washing machine, the whirring of the fan oven and the gentle hum of the computer. We are surrounded by noise. Some people find it easy to either block out noise or remain focused in a noisy environment. Others find it more difficult, and for them personal prayer can be an uphill struggle.

Many people today query the need for silence. We can pray to God wherever we are and whatever we are doing; we don't need to be still. God can and does speak to us through other people, through music, or through books. Why do we need to be still? Jesus shows us the importance of retreating from the busyness. In Mark 1:35, we read about Jesus getting up early in the morning and going to find a place where he could be alone to pray. Later on, we read that Jesus and the apostles are surrounded by so many people that they don't even have time to eat. They leave in a boat for a place where they can be alone (6:31–33). Mark tells us also that Jesus took Peter, James and John with him up a high mountain where they could be alone (9:2). Finally, on the night before he died, Jesus went to the garden of Gethsemane with his disciples. He walked a short distance from them so that he could be on his own to pray (14:32–36). If Jesus needed to spend time on his own in silence before God, then surely we do also.

Many of us have forgotten or were never taught how to use silence. We often long for silence and acknowledge the need to retreat from busyness, but when we get the opportunity we don't know how to use the silence. The quiet corners suggested in this book aim to help all of us discover or rediscover how to be silent before God and use that time constructively. Helping our children to meet with God in silence may be one of the most enduring gifts we can give them.

Where can we have a quiet corner?

A quiet corner can be set up in a church, a church hall, a school, at home, or even outdoors. You may decide to create a small corner around a single theme or, if a large space is available, you may like to create several separate prayer stations.

At my home church we have a corner set up close to the entrance. It has a pebble pool and a post-it prayer board. This rural church is always open and the small congregation have been so encouraged to see pebbles in the pool every week and occasional post-it prayers on the noticeboard. These symbols of prayer are placed on the Communion table every Sunday. It is good to see prayers written by children as well as adults. On occasions it has been a real privilege to observe parents and children holding pebbles and praying together at the pebble pool. The people and situations represented by the pebbles and the prayers written on the post-it notes are included in the intercessions at Sunday worship, together with prayers for the people who have prayed in church during the week. The small faithful congregation are encouraged to know that they are part of a much larger prayer community. The visitors are also encouraged to know that they are contributing and being drawn into the prayer life of the church. That, of course, is the purpose of the quiet corner: to lead people into prayer.

A series of multisensory prayer corners could also be set up around a church or cathedral. When we visit ancient churches and cathedrals, there is often a great deal of information about the history of the building but sometimes little that draws people into prayer. There is usually a side chapel set aside for private prayer, but this can be quite threatening for people who are unused to silent prayer. We tend to assume that prayer comes naturally, but many people find praying difficult. For many children today, their only experience of prayer is to respond with 'Amen' to someone else's prayers in a school assembly. A multisensory quiet area may help individuals of all ages take their first tentative steps into private and personal prayer.

When you know that several people may use the quiet area at the same time, and where space allows, it can be beneficial to turn a whole room into a quiet corner, placing different prayer stations around the room. This allows greater flexibility and choice for the participants. The idea has proved particularly effective at conferences, both day and residential, providing a quiet place of retreat from the busyness. It would adapt to a church weekend away or a mission event encouraging newcomers to pray. It could also be used for a day of prayer in a church or church hall, encouraging people to pray in different ways and challenging their traditional approach to prayer.

Another idea would be to offer to set up a quiet corner in school for children to use at lunchtime. If supervision is a problem, perhaps a quiet area could be set up in a corner of the school playground where staff and helpers are on hand to oversee its use. Prayers using pebbles and a small, non-glass pebble pool may be possible outdoors, or, if not, it may be possible to make a prayer cairn with pebbles.

To make a prayer cairn, choose large, flat pebbles and place them in some wicker baskets or garden trugs. In a flat area, lay a piece of strong canvas or hessian fabric on the ground. Place the baskets or trugs containing the pebbles at the edge of the fabric. Select some of the material in the 'Praying for others' quiet corner (see pages 68–72), but direct the children to build their pebbles into a cairn (a mound) instead of using a pebble pool. As some of the material for the prayer pool contains references to water, you may prefer to substitute the following Bible readings.

Join with me in praising the wonderful name of the Lord our God. The Lord is a mighty rock.
DEUTERONOMY 32:3–4A

You are my mighty rock, my fortress, my protector, the rock where I am safe, my shield... and my place of shelter.
PSALM 18:2

Let my words and my thoughts be pleasing to you, Lord, because you are my mighty rock and my protector.
PSALM 19:14

Prayer cards and additional materials would have to be laminated or adapted to protect them from the weather.

A quiet corner could also be set up at home. If space is at a premium and it is not possible to have a permanent arrangement, then some of the suggested themes lend themselves well to easy storage. Take, for example, the theme of the cross. This could be set up in a shiny silver gift box from a stationer's shop, lined with red felt. Inside this box you could keep a collection of crosses and pictures of crosses. If you keep the box with a piece of purple fabric, when you want to create a quiet corner simply lay out the purple cloth and open the box.

The opportunities for setting up a quiet corner are limitless, from portable materials in a shoebox to a station in a full-sized hall or church.

Using the quiet corners in this book

This book contains 14 quiet corners for you to choose from. You do not need to use them in any particular order. Each idea is self-contained and stands alone, so you can use just one, or you might choose to group two or three together.

The meditations are designed to guide the participant. You may want to leave copies of the book in the quiet corner, open at the appropriate chapter so that individuals can move at their own pace. Alternatively, you may wish to accompany children on their journey and read the reflective material out aloud. If you choose this route, be aware of pacing and spacing the material to allow the children time for personal reflection.

✣

Health and safety

Care must be taken to ensure the well-being of those using the quiet corner. The premises should be safe and well lit. Equipment should also be safe and appropriate to the age and ability of those using it. Further guidelines on particular objects, such as pebbles and candles, are given elsewhere in the book.

Those who are responsible for supervising children must have clearance from the Criminal Records Bureau. This should be organized through the school or church where the quiet corner is to be situated. Leaders should be aware of the church or school policy on touching children in their care. The Churches' Child Protection Advisory Service (CCPAS) has some helpful guidelines that are followed by many churches and organizations, including the Mothers' Union. In the prayerful atmosphere of a quiet corner, a child may feel prompted to talk about particular concerns, which may include abuse. It is vital that leaders are familiar with their church or school policy on child protection and know the procedures on how to react if a child wants to talk about abuse.

As with all children's activities, if parents or primary carers are not present, signed consent forms should be obtained containing the child's full name, date of birth, address, home and emergency contact telephone numbers, together with contact details of the family doctor, regular medication and ongoing medical problems, such as asthma, diabetes, allergies or special needs.

You may find the following websites useful:

www.everychildmatters.gov.uk   www.charity-commission.gov.uk
www.teachernet.gov.uk   www.crb.gov.uk
www.direct.gov.uk   www.ccpas.co.uk

✣

Preparation for quiet corners

Before getting started, you will need to identify where you are setting up your quiet corner and whether you are providing a single prayer station in a small corner or several stations in a larger area. You will also need to think about who will use the quiet corner. If you are creating a corner for a specific group of people, you may want to tailor the materials to take account of the age and ability of your group. You will also need to determine whether the quiet corner will be supervised or whether there will be open access, as this raises additional questions about health and safety concerns and child protection issues (see page 15).

Pictures

Many of the suggestions for quiet corners involve a collection of pictures. There are some excellent resources available to purchase from art galleries, bookshops and local gift shops, but you may want to supplement them with additional pictures that are appropriate for your location. For example, if you are setting up a quiet corner on the theme of the cross, you may want to include pictures of crosses in your own area. They may be available as postcards or you may prefer to use a digital camera and take photographs of crosses in your church or in your locality. You may also be fortunate in knowing a local artist who may be happy to draw or paint some pictures for you. Always aim for a wide variety and don't just choose pictures that you like. We all have different tastes and it is only fair to try to cater for a wide range of artistic preferences.

When gathering together a collection of pictures of people, do try to ensure that you create a good balance of age, gender, ethnicity, culture and environment. Other countries have a wide variety of living accommodation and work environments, just as our country has a wealth of towns, cities and rural communities. It is also good to create a positive view of disability by including pictures of individuals wearing spectacles or hearing aids or using wheelchairs. If you are planning to use photographs of local people, do ask their permission. Most people are only too pleased, but others may have good reason for not wanting their photographs on view.

The Internet is a good source of images. If you don't have access to a computer or are unsure about using the Internet, enlist the help of someone in your congregation or locality. People are usually very happy to help, if asked. Newspapers and magazines also provide a wealth of pictures, which can be cut out, mounted on cardboard and laminated so that they are hardwearing.

In some settings it may be appropriate to project a slideshow of images on a screen or wall, using a computer and projector. It is worth bearing in mind, however, that projected pictures cannot be held in the hand. Also, participants will not be able to set their own pace as the pictures change on a prearranged timescale.

Objects

Everything in a quiet corner is there to be handled, and this inevitably raises questions about safety (see page 15). If you are concerned about accidental damage to something precious, it is better not to use that item. Objects should, of course, be safe to handle, without small parts or sharp edges. There is inevitably a risk in using objects like pebbles in a pebble pool, but risks can be minimized by ensuring the that pebbles are large enough not to be swallowed by young children and that the children are closely supervised. Damage may be caused by pebbles being thrown, but with appropriate adult supervision this problem should be easy to overcome.

Health and safety is of paramount importance and, with care and forethought, it should be possible to anticipate problems and ensure that accidents do not occur. It is much better to use real objects than to be cocooned in an artificially safe environment, and being aware of inherent risks will ensure that everyone is kept safe.

Bible focus cards

It is helpful to have the words of the Bible focus written out on a card so that they can be easily seen and read. The passages are mostly short and can be easily printed out on to thin card and laminated, so that they are durable. If you do not have access to a laminator, local business suppliers often have this facility available. The Contemporary English Version of the Bible has been used throughout this book, but Bible verses in a range of different versions of the Bible can be found on the Internet. For example, visit www.biblegateway.com.

Candles

Candles are often associated with prayer and basic safety measures need to be in place wherever and whenever candles are used. Tealights should always be in holders on a metal tray or embedded in damp sand. Always place candles in holders well out of reach of the children. Floating candles in a prayer pool can be very effective, but should be closely supervised, even though they are surrounded by water. Children can be allowed to light candles, but will require careful oversight when doing so. Have ready a candle snuffer to extinguish the candles, a bucket of water for emergencies, and a bucket of damp sand in which to place the candles after use. Never leave lighted candles in an unsupervised area or unattended.

Food and drink

The use of food and drink in a quiet corner also raises potential difficulties because of the increase in the number of people suffering from food allergies. If you have responsibility for a group of children, you will need to have specific details of allergies and avoid contact with those foods. Common allergies include nuts, wheat and dairy, and these foods should be avoided if possible. Artificial food colourings also cause problems for many children so these too should be avoided.

Craft materials

Many of the quiet corners include a suggested craft activity so sufficient materials for that activity will be needed. You may find it helpful to provide additional templates and activity suggestions to support the theme of your quiet corner. It can be useful to have an area set aside with basic craft materials, such as paper, card, wool, ribbon, thread, crayons, self-hardening clay or playdough, glue, child-safety scissors and so on, so that individuals can respond in their own way. A plastic toolbox with different sections can be an effective way of keeping materials tidy yet available, and ensures that the craft area does not overwhelm or dominate the quiet corner. Additional craft materials needed for individual quiet corners are listed under the 'Getting started' section of each unit.

Books and Bibles

It can be helpful to provide one or two books supporting the theme of the prayer corner, again taking into account the age and ability of participants. There are many excellent storybooks that help to make the Bible accessible to children. A well-illustrated book, such as

The Barnabas Children's Bible (Barnabas, 2007) or *My First Bible* (Barnabas, 2006), can add a fresh perspective to a traditional Bible story. A Bible in a modern translation, such as *The Global Bible for Children* (Authentic, 2005) and a children's Bible, such as those mentioned above, can be useful additions for those who prefer to spend part of their quiet time reading. Sometimes the Bible reading can be enhanced by having a different version of the Bible, as, for example, in the corner about the good shepherd where time is spent reflecting on Psalm 23 (see pages 85–86). You may find that individuals will be encouraged to read more of the Bible passage if you lay the Bible open at the correct passage for the Bible focus.

Poems and writing

Some people respond well to poetry and prose, so it is often a good idea to try to include a poem or a piece of writing to help develop thought around the Bible focus. There is a wealth of great literature to choose from, but one of the best sources is your local school or church congregation. Many school display boards feature one or more pieces of creative writing that show remarkable insight and give a fresh perspective. You may find that an individual using a prayer corner will choose to respond to their quiet time with God by writing a piece of poetry and leaving it there to inspire others. Don't forget, also, that the words of hymns and worship songs can be used to prompt thoughts and help generate a response to the Bible focus.

Music

Music is so personal to individuals that it is often better to choose not to provide music in a quiet corner. Primarily, the purpose of a quiet corner is to draw people into silence, giving an opportunity to meet and listen to God. However, if the prayer space is only going to be used by one person at a time, you may decide to make a CD player available, together with an assortment of CDs so that people can make their own choice. Another alternative is to provide personal CD players with headphones.

Other sounds

Sounds of nature may be used to support a theme. For example, you might wish to consider providing an indoor water fountain to support a theme, such as the good shepherd leading his sheep to quiet waters, or a basket of autumn leaves that rustle when a hand is dipped in for the quiet corner on creation.

Presentation

The presentation of materials is important, as the aim of the quiet corner is to draw individuals into a quality time with God. Time spent in the quiet corner is worship and we should be aiming to bring our best to God.

All of the suggestions for quiet corners in this book are arranged on fabric, draped either over a table top or on the floor. The right fabric provides texture and colour and can help to bring the materials to life. End-of-roll oddments from your local fabric store are easy to obtain and not expensive to buy. Charity shops and town market stalls are also good sources of fabrics that can usually be purchased fairly cheaply.

It is also helpful to collect together an assortment of containers for small items. The use of bowls and boxes gives a sense of order to the quiet corner and also makes it easier to present materials neatly. Pebbles can look more attractive and inviting to touch when they are arranged in a wicker or wooden bowl. Stars and other small items can be kept tidily in small decorative boxes.

All components of a quiet corner are meant to be handled, so inevitably some may begin to look tired and frayed around the edges. Most of the materials are readily available and easy to replace, but you may find it worthwhile to stock up on certain items when you can. For example, silver stars are easier to find around Christmas time and they are often significantly reduced in price in the post-Christmas sales. Also, heart-shaped items are readily available around Valentine's Day but are hard to find at other times of year. It is well worth laminating pictures and pieces of writing, as this significantly extends their life.

The best advice is to try to keep each quiet area simple. It can be tempting to put too much into a corner to try to cater for everyone, but the results can be overwhelming and not conducive to stillness and quietness.

How to use this book

This book contains everything you need to set up and run a quiet corner. Each chapter comprises a range of different elements designed to guide the participant through the material. You may find it helpful to leave copies of the book in the quiet corner, open at the correct page, so that people can use the material at their own pace.

Getting started

This section provides information about all the materials you need to set up the quiet corner, and suggestions for how to arrange and display fabrics, pictures and objects. Additional craft materials for specific quiet corners are also listed.

Stilling

All of the suggestions for quiet corners have ideas for stilling—bringing the mind and body to a point of stillness—so that we are not only more ready to talk to God but also more prepared to listen. Some people can settle quite quickly into a quiet time with God; others take longer. When using the quiet corner, some people may only get as far as the stilling activity, while others may move quickly to the Bible focus and beyond. The emphasis is for each participant to move at his or her own pace and allow the Holy Spirit to lead. As participants get used to becoming still, it tends to become easier to move into stillness and individuals may well be surprised by the directions in which God leads them.

Helping children to be still

It may be helpful to provide guidance to help children to relax. Ask the child to prepare for being quiet by relaxing their body and letting their shoulders drop a little. Ask them to make sure they feel comfortable, to close their eyes and think about their breathing, making it slow and steady. Some may find it helpful to pray the name Jesus silently, breathing in on the first syllable and out on the second. Ask them to listen to the sounds in the room for a few moments. What noises can they hear? Ask them to keep still and focused. It may be helpful for them to close their eyes and make a picture in their head that is about the story, or to focus on an object with their eyes open, or to hold an object in their hand.

Bible focus

All the multisensory activities in a quiet corner aim to support and develop the theme echoed in the Bible focus. In his first letter, the apostle John observes, 'The Word that gives life was from the beginning, and this is the one our message is about. Our ears have heard, our own eyes have seen, and our hands touched this Word' (1 John 1:1). As we take time in the stillness to reflect on God's word using our senses, and as we allow the Holy Spirit to be active within us, the Bible comes alive with meaning and purpose.

As mentioned in the Introduction, it is helpful to have the Bible focus printed out on card and laminated. However, it is also important to have a Bible available so that participants can read around the passage or explore the Bible further as the Holy Spirit leads them.

Staying with the story

This section aims to provide more resources to support and develop our thinking about the Bible focus. There may be some additional passages from the Bible to reflect on, or some poetry or prose. It is up to you to choose the extra materials you wish to provide, as they will be determined by the age and ability of the people who will use your quiet corner. There is a wealth of resources available, but it is advisable to be selective as it is possible to overwhelm the quiet area and make it feel too busy. If you are planning to leave a quiet corner in place for some time, you could ring the changes by removing some items and replacing them with others. Some of the suggestions for quiet corners include an activity to supplement and enhance this time of reflection on the Bible focus. You may well come up with other ideas: don't be afraid to experiment.

Living with the story

This section provides a concrete activity to reinforce and ground the theme of the quiet corner. The suggestions are not prescriptive but offer enough alternatives to encourage a response from the most uncreative while not limiting the imagination of the more creative individual. It can be helpful to provide templates to get people started, and also to provide additional craft materials so that individuals can continue to respond according to how the Holy Spirit is leading them. Do not be tempted to intervene and help if you are supervising children. It is important to remember that this creative response is still part of the prayer time and is personal between God and the individual.

Prayer response

Nearly all of the time spent in the quiet corner is for prayer. We are drawn into stillness by touching and looking at objects and pictures. We spend time reflecting on God's word. We can choose whether to respond verbally or non-verbally and allow space for God to speak to us. These are all different aspects of prayer. The prayer response may prompt further prayer or it may be used to bring the session to a close.

Living the journey

This section takes the theme beyond the quiet corner and seeks to make relevant connections to our everyday life. Worship is an important element of the Christian faith, but we are called to live out our faith wherever we are. As James asks in his letter addressed to Christians scattered all over the world, 'What good is it to say you have faith, when you don't do anything to show that you really do have faith?' (James 2:14).

Once again, the ideas in this section are only suggestions. Individuals may find that God is speaking to them in a specific way and drawing them to make an alternative response.

✜

The labyrinth

The preparation for the quiet corner 'The journey' (see pages 73–77) involves making a finger labyrinth out of clay. This can be done quite quickly, although extra time will be needed to make sure that the clay is fully dry before painting or varnishing the finished labyrinth.

Before making a finger labyrinth, it is well worth taking time to explore the background to the labyrinth and gain an understanding of the labyrinth as a spiritual tool. If you have not encountered the concept before, it is best described as a means to help develop a life of prayer. Many people discover that the preparation leading up to walking a full-sized labyrinth or using a finger labyrinth is a significant part of their spiritual journey.

Making your own labyrinth can be an important part of the experience. Instructions are given below for making a finger labyrinth. However, once you have experienced the benefits of using a labyrinth, you may feel inspired to widen your horizons.

The first full-sized labyrinth I made was on the Cefn Sidan beach in Carmarthenshire, West Wales. I chose a place on the beach where the sand was reasonably firm and selected a piece of driftwood with which to draw. I began by drawing the base pattern; before long all the lines were connected and my Cretan labyrinth was complete. Before entering the labyrinth, I paused and asked God's blessing on my walk. As the path led me near to and then further from the centre, I began to see the labyrinth as a reflection of life's journey—how the times when I have felt far away from God have ultimately brought me closer. As I walked on, all the cares and concerns of daily life seemed to be lifted from me and as I arrived at the centre of the labyrinth I felt an overwhelming sense of peace. Time seemed to stand still.

As I prepared to move away from the centre, I left the piece of driftwood standing upright in the sand as an offering to God. During the outward walk, I felt strengthened, encouraged and valued. As I approached the exit, I turned to walk out backwards, aware of leaving sacred space.

If you don't have access to a beach, you could make a temporary labyrinth in the playground at your local school or in the grounds of your local church using pavement chalk. If there is space in the school or church hall, you could mark out a labyrinth using masking tape and make it available for the duration of a holiday club.

I have a grass labyrinth in my garden, with the pathway of the labyrinth cut shorter than the surrounding grass. The possibilities are limited only by imagination.

History and background to the labyrinth

The labyrinth is firmly rooted in Christian history, although labyrinths were originally pre-Christian. Possibly the oldest surviving one can be found in a rock carving at Luzzanas in Sardinia and dates from between 2500 and 2000BC. The earliest Christian labyrinth is thought to be the one found in the fourth-century basilica of Repartus, Orleansville in Algeria.

Typically, a labyrinth measures a minimum of twelve metres in diameter and is designed for walking. The traditional understanding involves a journey of three parts: walking in, spending time at the centre and then walking out.

There are two main forms of labyrinth: the Cretan and the Chartres. The Cretan—the oldest form, dating back at least 3500 years—is named after the island of Crete where, according to ancient myth, the Minotaur lived in an underground labyrinth. However, this mythical labyrinth was actually a maze, because the Minotaur couldn't find its way out. A maze is designed to confuse, with lots of dead ends and detours, whereas a labyrinth has only one pathway in and the same pathway out. The classical seven-circuit Cretan labyrinth provides the model for almost all forms apart from the Chartres design. The Chartres labyrinth takes its name from the permanent design set into the stone floor of Chartres Cathedral in France. It is dated between 1194 and 1220 and is approximately 13 metres in diameter.

The roots of Christianity lie in the Jewish religion and its associated pilgrim festivals. The tradition of pilgrimage to the holy land went on developing right up to the Crusades, which began in 1095. During the Crusades, when the pilgrimage to Jerusalem became too dangerous, the Roman Catholic Church appointed designated cathedrals to become the symbolic Jerusalem for pilgrims. The labyrinths at these cathedrals were often known as the 'Road to Jerusalem' and the centre was called the New Jerusalem. Walking the labyrinth marked the completion of the pilgrimage.

The earliest labyrinth seen on a wall is believed to be at St Lucca Cathedral in Italy and dates from the ninth century. This finger labyrinth has a diameter of about 45cm. It was designed for people to trace with their fingers and the idea was to quieten their mind so that they would enter the cathedral in a prayerful attitude.

Modern-day labyrinths

In the last few years, there has been a resurgence of interest in the use of the labyrinth as an aid to prayer. Many modern-day labyrinths have been designed around a series of prayer stations, which people enter and leave at their own pace. At other labyrinths, participants are provided with a commentary and music through personal headphones to accompany them on their journey. However, the labyrinth referred to in the quiet corner 'The journey' is a classical labyrinth without prayer stations.

The benefits of the finger labyrinth

Walking a labyrinth can be time-consuming, not least because most people have to travel quite a distance to visit one. Also, to gain the most out of walking the labyrinth, there needs to be adequate preparation and an open-ended period of time. I remember visiting a grass labyrinth on my way to an appointment. It was beautifully cut into a Chartres design, a masterpiece of craftsmanship. My time was limited but nevertheless I decided to walk the labyrinth. However, the walk was disappointing because I wasn't really aware of God's presence. Thinking back, I realized that I hadn't prepared for the walk: the decision had been on the spur of the moment and I was walking under pressure of time. It had been a physical rather than spiritual exercise.

The finger labyrinth provides an easier and more accessible method. It is portable so it can be used anywhere and at any time. It is walked with the fingers, so it can be used by people with reduced mobility who may find walking a full-sized labyrinth physically challenging. The distance travelled along the path of a finger labyrinth is much shorter than for the full-sized walking labyrinth and so requires less time.

Drawing the labyrinth

Before you can make a finger labyrinth, you will need to draw the pattern of the labyrinth. Drawing the basic pattern is not difficult, but you may need time and practice before you find yourself able to draw it freehand. You may like to work quietly on your own or you may like to work with a small group. Drawing the labyrinth is an appropriate activity for people of all ages, although very young children may require assistance. Make this a special time by praying before you start, asking God for the gifts of patience and creativity. You may like to play some gentle reflective music as you work.

Before you start, read the following words from John 8:6: 'They asked Jesus this question, because they wanted to test him and bring some charge against him. But Jesus simply bent over and started writing on the ground with his finger.'

Jesus had been asked a difficult question. John doesn't tell us why Jesus wrote on the ground, or what he wrote, but this unique account creates a strong image in the mind as we think about Jesus' action.

- Think about what Jesus may have written…
- Think about why he chose to write…
- Think about the time and space that writing can create. Perhaps Jesus wanted time to think before he replied…

As you spend time drawing, what do you need to think about? Clear your mind of all extraneous thoughts and let your drawing become a prayer.

Begin by drawing the base pattern on paper. Notice that the centre of the labyrinth is below the centre of your page, so start to draw about a third of the way up from the bottom of your paper and slightly left of centre (see diagram 1 overleaf). You may find it helpful to use squared paper to start with. Lightly write numbers in pencil corresponding to the numbers in the diagram (see diagram 2).

Beginning with the left-hand number one, join both lines marked with a number one with a sweeping curve (see diagram 2). This forms the centre of the labyrinth.

Continue to link matching numbers with sweeping curves. Always start with the left-hand number and go over the top of the centre. When you have finished, your labyrinth pattern should be the same as in diagram 3. As you draw the labyrinth, notice the cross in the centre and the way that the cross extends into a shepherd's crook.

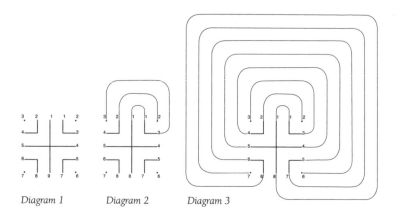

Diagram 1   Diagram 2   Diagram 3

When you are comfortable with drawing the labyrinth freehand on paper, set your work to one side. Spend some time thanking God for the space and time for quiet reflection. If you are working with a group, conclude the session with a closing prayer.

Making the labyrinth

Making a clay finger labyrinth can also be done individually or in a group setting. When working with a group, it is very interesting to see how each completed labyrinth is unique and subtly reflects the character of its creator.

> **You will need:** Pencil and paper, self-hardening clay, a rolling-pin, waxed paper, water, a tray or board for the finished labyrinth, and paint or varnish.

Before you begin to work with the clay, draw a labyrinth on paper. This will be the pattern for your finger labyrinth and you may need to refer to it as you work.

Reflect on the following words from Isaiah 64:8 as you begin to work with the clay: 'You, Lord, are our Father. We are nothing but clay, but you are the potter who moulded us.' Use the following thoughts to guide your reflection.

■ Think about the things in your life that God is seeking to change...
■ Think about God moulding you to bring about those changes...

First of all, knead the clay to remove any air bubbles and then roll it flat into an oval shape measuring approximately 30cm by 25cm.

Mark the outline of the labyrinth with a pencil, making sure the pathway is wide enough for the width of your middle finger. When you are happy with the outline, begin at the centre and use your fingers to mould the pathway and build up the walls. If you find that the clay becomes too thin, you may find it easier to prepare the flat base and then use snakes of coiled clay to mark out the labyrinth pattern. In this way, you will be able to get the basic pattern right and then form the path by smoothing the coiled clay into the base.

Don't worry if your first attempt has to be kneaded back into a block, or if you run out of space on one side when drawing the outline or forming it out of coiled clay. Keep persevering until you have a base that feels right and an outline that is pleasing to the eye. When you are happy with the basic shape, start at the centre and use your fingers to mould the pathway and build up the walls between the tracks. Time and again allow your fingers to return to the cross at the centre and the reassurance of the shepherd's crook before following the path towards the entrance. Allow the cares and pressures of the day to drift away as you become absorbed in working the clay.

When you have finished working on your labyrinth, set it aside on a board to dry completely. Spend some time quietly thanking

God for the time of reflection. If you have been working in a group, conclude the session with a closing prayer.

Your finger labyrinth can be painted and varnished when it is completely dry. Children will need adult help and close supervision when painting or varnishing.

Walking the labyrinth

After using a finger labyrinth, you may want to encourage your group to walk a full-sized labyrinth. You may be fortunate in having one near you but, if not, you might like to try making your own.

Quiet corners

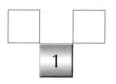

Jesus is... the true vine

In this quiet corner we begin by thinking about trees and how they grow. This leads in to thoughts about gardeners, raising awareness of God as gardener and creator. Choosing and holding a leaf can help to create a sense of awe and wonder, as each leaf is different from every other leaf and contains its own intricate pattern of veins. This sense of awe and wonder can naturally lead into a time of gratitude, expressing thanks to God for all the good things in life.

The Bible focus reinforces the idea of God as gardener and turns our attention to Jesus. Jesus said, 'I am the true vine' (John 15:1) so we use images and words to help us understand what Jesus meant. This leads to reflection on the work of the Holy Spirit and the fruit of the Spirit.

Spending time contemplating the role of God as creator encourages a respect for the environment and stimulates awareness of the wonder of life and creation. Delving deeper into the image of Jesus as the vine and the role of the Holy Spirit can give us a clearer idea of who we are and how we can grow to be more like Jesus.

Getting started

Arrange some twigs in a plant pot to make a tree. Stand the plant pot on some brown fabric to represent the soil. Place the following items near the plant pot.

- Some pictures of trees
- Some leaves
- A basket containing sticky tack and small green pieces of paper for leaves
- A basket containing drawing paper, pencils, child-safe scissors and glue sticks
- A bowl of seedless grapes
- A picture of a grape vine, or a grape vine growing in a pot (available from some garden centres)
- A card with the words from Galatians 5:22–23: 'God's Spirit makes us loving, happy, peaceful, patient, kind, good, faithful, gentle, and self-controlled.'
- Cards with the words from the 'Staying with the story' section (see pages 38–39)

Stilling

Spend some time quietly looking at the pictures of trees.

Choose the picture you like best and think about the tree... the soil it grows in...

Think about what a tree needs to help it grow... sunlight, warmth, rain...

Think about a young tree, a sapling, and the gardener who plants it in the ground. The gardener tends the tree, giving it food and water, and watches it grow. Gardeners take delight in watching their trees grow...

Think about God as a gardener, how he takes delight in everything that he has created, how he wants you to delight in everything that he has created...

Choose a leaf and hold it in your hand as you spend some time quietly saying 'thank you' to God for all the things you enjoy.

Bible focus

Jesus said to his disciples, 'I am the true vine, and my Father is the gardener.'
JOHN 15:1

Look at the picture of the grape vine.

Think about the vine… the soil it grows in… its roots… its trunk… its branches … its fruit…

Think about the sap flowing through the vine… from the roots… into the trunk… into the branches…

Think about Jesus as the vine… and the Holy Spirit flowing through the vine…

Think of yourself as a branch in that vine and the Holy Spirit flowing through you…

Staying with the story

Jesus said, 'Stay joined to me, and I will stay joined to you. Just as a branch cannot produce fruit unless it stays joined to the vine, you cannot produce fruit unless you stay joined to me. I am the vine, and you are the branches. If you stay joined to me, and I stay joined to you, then you will produce lots of fruit. But you cannot do anything without me.'
JOHN 15:4–5

Plant your roots in Christ and let him be the foundation for your life. Be strong in your faith, just as you were taught. And be grateful.
COLOSSIANS 2:7

Jesus says, 'I am the vine, and you are the branches.' The Holy Spirit flows through Jesus just as the sap flows through the grape vine. You are one of the branches joined to Jesus, and the Holy Spirit flows through you just as the Holy Spirit flows through Jesus. The vine produces fruit and the Holy Spirit produces fruit in you.

God's Spirit makes us loving, happy, peaceful, patient, kind, good, faithful, gentle, and self-controlled.
GALATIANS 5:22–23

Think about the fruit of the Spirit as you taste one of the grapes.

Living with the story

Cut out and colour some circle shapes to look like grapes and write one of the fruits of the Spirit in each circle.

■ Love
■ Happiness
■ Peace
■ Patience
■ Kindness
■ Goodness
■ Faithfulness
■ Gentleness
■ Self-control

As you cut and write, think about the fruit of the Spirit one at a time. Ask God to help the fruit of the Spirit to grow in you. Listen to God as ideas come into your mind. For example, God may suggest ways in which you could do something kind for someone in your family. Draw a branch on a piece of paper and stick your circle shapes on it so that they look like a bunch of grapes.

Keep the bunch of grapes you have made in a special place. Keep asking God to grow the fruit of the Spirit in you. Keep listening for God's suggestions.

Cut a leaf shape out of green paper and write your name on it. Place it in the picture of a grape vine or fasten it to a branch of the growing vine, as a sign that you are part of the vine and that you want to stay close to Jesus.

Prayer response

Loving God, thank you for sending your Holy Spirit to help me. Please help me to become more like Jesus every day. Amen

Living the journey

Try one or more of the following activities.

- Visit a garden centre to look at different sorts of trees and plants. Look closely at leaves and flowers and think about how God must have enjoyed creating the world.
- Grow some plants of your own. You could buy a packet of seeds in the garden centre or you could plant some orange or lemon pips.
- Do a kind deed every day.

2

The cross

This quiet corner gives an opportunity to explore our understanding of the cross. The symbolism of the cross can be quite confusing; this is reflected in the Bible focus from 1 Corinthians 1:18, which explains that the cross makes no sense to some people and yet, to others, it is God's power at work.

In daily life, a cross can indicate a wrong answer, yet on a voting paper a cross indicates the person you want to vote for. A cross can say 'not this way' but it can also warn of an impending road junction, giving opportunities for choice. Crosses are often viewed as an art form and can be ornate or simple. They are often used on necklaces and earrings as jewellery, as well as symbolizing the Christian faith. They can be seen inside and outside churches, as an empty cross or a crucifix. The empty cross reveals Christ's triumph over death, while the crucifix reminds us of Christ's suffering and the way he identifies with the suffering of the world. Although the cross was a form of execution, for Christians the cross is a symbol not of death but of life.

In this quiet corner we begin by thinking about the use of crosses in everyday life. As we think of crosses on road signs warning of road junctions and signs at crossroads showing the way, we begin to see the cross as a signpost, showing us the way to live. The Bible focus turns our attention to the Christian understanding of the cross. There is an opportunity to look at and feel crosses of many designs while reading words of well-known hymns, worship songs or Bible passages. Taking time to reflect on the cross can lead to a more profound understanding of Jesus' sacrificial love and draw us into a deeper relationship with Jesus.

Getting started

Collect some pictures of crosses in different situations, such as road signs, a cross against a wrong answer and a cross on a voting paper, and arrange them on a tray.

Collect a variety of crosses of all shapes and sizes, such as palm crosses, bookmarks, jewellery and ornate and simple wooden crosses, and arrange them on a tray lined with red fabric.

Place both trays on purple fabric draped over a table top or on the floor. Surround the trays with pictures of crosses. *A-cross the World* by Martyn Payne and Betty Pedley (Barnabas, 2004) is a good source. Visit www.barnabasinchurches.org.uk/pages/2877.htm.

Place the words of a hymn or worship song about the cross among the pictures. For example, you might choose 'The wondrous cross' by Isaac Watts, 'There is a green hill far away' by C.F. Alexander, 'Saviour of the world' by Greg Leavers (*Junior Praise* 216), or 'The servant king' by Graham Kendrick (*The Source* 114).

Have the craft box ready, but include some natural items such as small twigs, string, wool, fabrics such as hessian, playdough or self-hardening clay, and handmade papers (available from craft shops or stationery shops such as Paperchase: www.paperchase.co.uk).

Stilling

God loved the people of this world so much that he gave his only Son, so that everyone who has faith in him will have eternal life and never really die.
JOHN 3:16

Spend some time quietly looking at the pictures of crosses in different situations...

Think about what the different crosses mean...

Imagine a world without road signs warning us about what lies ahead... think about how dangerous the roads would be...

Without road signs, how would we know which way to go...?

How we would learn if we didn't know if our answers were right or wrong...?

Hold one of the signs in your hand as you quietly spend some time thanking God for all the signs that help to keep us safe, and all the signs that help us to learn the right way to go...

Bible focus

The message about the cross doesn't make any sense to lost people. But for those of us who are being saved, it is God's power at work.
1 CORINTHIANS 1:18

Look at the crosses on the tray.

Look at the different colours, patterns and pictures on the crosses.

Feel the different textures.

Think about which one you like best.

Think about why you like this one best.

Think about which one you like least.

Think about why you like this one least.

Staying with the story

Choose one of the crosses and hold it in your hand as you think about the words from one of the hymns or worship songs or from the Bible.

43

God loved the people of this world so much that he gave his only Son, so that everyone who has faith in him will have eternal life and never really die.
JOHN 3:16

Think of the words, just a few at a time, and close your eyes as you feel the surface of the cross. Keep thinking of those same words, saying them to yourself again and again as you feel the shape of the cross.

Living with the story

Use some of the craft materials to make your own cross.

You may like to draw a simple cross on paper or cardboard and decorate it with flowers or Christian symbols.

You may like to make a cross out of playdough or self-hardening clay. You could make it rough or smooth.

You may like to write some words from the Bible on your cross.

You may like to weave a cross with strips of paper, fabric or wool.

Prayer response

Lord Jesus, thank you for dying on the cross and rising to new life. Please help me be aware of your love always surrounding me. Amen

Living the journey

Try one or more of the following activities.

- Visit a local church to look at all the different sorts of crosses inside the church and in the churchyard.

- Christians in different countries and cultures often have their own special versions of the cross. Find out about different crosses from around the world. Look for different patterns and designs and the stories behind them. You could look in library books, talk to people in your local church, or do some research on the Internet.
- Using natural items such as small twigs, wool or handmade paper, make some different crosses and start your own collection.

3

Jesus is... the light for the world

In this quiet corner we begin by thinking about light. When we consider the numerous sources of light, we begin to appreciate how important it is to us and how different life would be without it. As we think also about the sun and moon as sources of light, we turn once again to God our creator and give him thanks for the gift of light.

The Bible focus turns our attention to Jesus, who said, 'I am the light for the world' (John 8:12), and we begin to reflect on what Jesus meant by this statement. Dark material and shiny blank CDs provide a good contrast between light and dark, as the CDs catch the available light and reflect it back. The use of a torch on the CDs enhances the contrast and can help us to understand the concept of light shining in the darkness. The illustration would be even more effective in a darkened room. This understanding can then be grounded in our world as we identify places on a map of the world with which we are familiar, either through personal contact or through news items. (Care should be taken when selecting news items to make sure that good news is represented alongside areas of concern.) Placing silver stars on the world map to represent these places and shining a torch on them to make them sparkle gives a wonderfully vivid image of Jesus as the light for the world.

Getting started

Arrange dark-coloured fabric on a table top or on the floor to represent the night sky. Place a lantern-type torch in the middle of a shiny metal tray and place the tray on the dark fabric.

Collect pictures of light sources, such as a lighthouse, car headlights, a torch, candles, fire, the sun and the moon, and arrange them around the edge of the dark fabric.

Place on the dark fabric a card with the words from Genesis 1:16, 'God made two powerful lights, the brighter one to rule the day and the other to rule the night.'

Place a large map of the world on the floor or table top.

Place a box of shiny stars next to the map of the world.

Place some blank CDs on the dark fabric.

Place some current headlines from newspapers on a tray to one side of the world map.

Stilling

Spend some time quietly looking at the pictures of lights.

Think about how each light is used...

Think about how helpful each light is and what might happen if that light was not there...

Look at the picture of the sun and think about the warmth and light it gives us...

Look at the picture of the moon and think about the gentle light it brings during the night...

As you look at the pictures of the sun and moon, read the following words from Genesis 1:16: 'God made two powerful lights, the brighter one to rule the day and the other to rule the night.'

Spend some time quietly saying 'thank you' to God for the gift of light, which helps to keep us safe and show us the way.

Bible focus

Jesus said, 'I am the light for the world! Follow me, and you won't be walking in the dark. You will have the light that gives life.'
JOHN 8:12

Think about the light that Jesus brings...

Think about some of the Bible stories you have heard about Jesus...

... how he healed people and changed their lives...

... how he taught people to care for one another...

... how he taught the disciples to pray...

Staying with the story

Think about these other words from the Bible.

The light keeps shining in the dark, and darkness has never put it out.
JOHN 1:5

God's love and kindness will shine upon us like the sun that rises in the sky.
LUKE 1:78

Place some CDs on the dark fabric. Look at the colours as they catch the light. Shine the torch on the CDs and watch them sparkle as they reflect the light from the torch. Think about yourself as the light of Jesus shines on you and as you reflect that light on to other people.

Living with the story

If you have friends or relatives living in faraway places, try to find those places on the world map.

If you have travelled overseas, try to find the places you have visited on the world map.

Look at the map of the world and try to find some places you have heard about in the news. Look at the news headlines on the tray to remind you of some of these places.

Place some shiny stars on the world map as you find all these places.

Shine the torch to make the stars sparkle and represent the light of Jesus shining in those places.

Prayer response

Lord Jesus, thank you for your light, which shines around the world. Please help me to show your light to others. Amen

Living the journey

Try one or more of the following activities.

- Make a mobile by tying blank CDs together. You could hang them in your bedroom to catch the light and remind you that Jesus is the light for the world.
- Try to see the good side of people rather than being critical of them.
- Smile more often. Smiles are infectious. You might encourage other people to smile more often, too.

The family of God

In this quiet corner we begin by thinking about the launch of a rocket into space. This leads into thoughts about the enormity of our universe and the countless stars and planets. Linking the awesomeness and enormity of our universe with the biblical account of creation in the Bible (Genesis 1:1—2:4) helps to raise our awareness of God as creator and can lead naturally into a time of worship, giving thanks to God for the wonder of all his creation.

The Bible focus links the magnitude of the stars in the sky with the story of God's promise to Abraham, that his descendants would be as numerous as those stars. We are part of that great family. The careful placement of stars on dark material helps us first of all to explore our relationships within our immediate family and then our relationships with friends and their families. As we gather our carefully placed stars together and reflect on God as creator, we begin to think of all the people who make up one large family with God at the head. As we scatter the stars, we can begin to think about where we are in that great family.

As we discovered in the quiet corner on 'Jesus... light for the world' (see pages 46–49), spending time contemplating on the role of God as creator helps to stimulate an awareness of the wonder and awe of life and our world. As we think about ourselves as being part of one great family of God, we can gain a greater sense of identity and belonging and develop a greater respect for other people.

Getting started

Arrange some dark fabric on the floor or table top to represent the night sky. Place a box of shiny stars (table confetti) to one side of the dark cloth. On the wall behind the fabric, arrange the following items:

- Pictures of the night sky, planets, and space rockets
- A card with the words from Genesis 1:16–18, 'God made two powerful lights, the brighter one to rule the day and the other to rule the night. He also made the stars. Then God put these lights in the sky to shine on the earth, to rule day and night, and to separate light from darkness. God looked at what he had done, and it was good.'

Collect in a basket some pictures of people of all ages and nationalities. Place the basket to one side of the dark cloth.

Stilling

Spend some time quietly looking at a picture of a space rocket...

Think about the space rocket being launched into the sky...

Think about how far a space rocket can travel...

Imagine the view from the space rocket, seeing the stars and the planets...

Think about what the planet earth looks like from space...

Think about how many stars there are in the sky...

Think about God creating the world. Read the words from the Bible on the card, telling us about God creating the stars in the sky.

Hold some stars in your hand and spend some time quietly thanking God for the wonder of our universe, for the stars and planets, for our own planet earth, and for all that God has created.

Bible focus

God promised Abraham, 'I will bless you and give you such a large family, that some day your descendants will be more numerous than the stars in the sky or the grains of sand along the beach.'
GENESIS 22:17A

Place a star on the dark cloth to represent you...

Place some more stars to represent members of your family—your parents, brothers, sisters, aunts, uncles, grandparents, cousins... Are all the stars close together or are some further away from your star...?

Place some more stars to represent your friends and the people in their families...

Spend some time thanking God for all the important people in your life, for all the people you love, and for all the people who love you.

Staying with the story

Take the pictures of people out of the basket...

Think about what their names might be...

Try to imagine the places they live...

Think about their families and friends...

Collect all your stars from the cloth and hold them in your hand...

Think again about God's promise to Abraham, that his descendants would be more numerous than the stars in the sky...

Think about being part of God's great family...

When you are ready, scatter your stars on the dark cloth to represent members of God's family all over the world.

Think about where your star is now...

Living with the story

Use some dark paper or fabric and make your own starry sky picture to remind you that we are all part of God's great family. You could use ready-made stars or you could make your own stars with shiny paper to show that we are all different.

Prayer response

Loving God, thank you for making us all part of one big family. Please help me to show love and concern for all your people everywhere. Amen

Living the journey

Try one or more of the following activities.

- If your church or school has overseas links, find out what life is like in that country.
- If someone at school speaks a different language at home, learn some words of welcome in that language.
- When you hear a country mentioned in the news, look on a map to find out where it is.

5

Names for Jesus

In this quiet corner we begin by looking in a mirror and thinking about ourselves. We think about the person we are, our relationships with others, the things we like to do. As part of who we are, we may also think about how others see us. This may lead us to think of something about ourselves that we are not happy with, that we might like to change. It may be something superficial like the colour of our hair or it may be a desire to control our temper. We may have concerns about parts of ourselves that we can't change, such as our height or the size of our feet. As we turn to God our creator and talk to him about how we view ourselves, we can begin to see ourselves as God sees us, created as individuals for a purpose and loved by God.

As our thoughts turn to Jesus with the Bible focus, we can see that he was also interested to know what other people thought about him. As we think about Jesus asking his disciples, 'Who do you say I am?' (Matthew 16:15) we can begin to think about our own answer to that question. It is tempting to use purple fabric as the base for this quiet corner, as purple reinforces the idea of kingship and supports Peter's response that Jesus is the Messiah. However, the use of multicoloured fabric combines with the pictures and descriptions to stretch the imagination so that we can think more widely about Jesus and gain a broader perspective and deeper understanding of who he is. As we learn more about Jesus, we allow ourselves to be drawn closer in our relationship with him.

Getting started

Arrange some bright multicoloured fabric on the floor or table top.
Place a mirror in the centre of the cloth.
Collect some pictures of Jesus and place them on the cloth.
Collect some written descriptions of Jesus. There are many in the Bible—for example, the light for the world (John 8:12), the good shepherd (10:14), the bread of life (6:35), and the true vine (15:1). Many people have written about Jesus: Mother Teresa talks of Jesus as her life and her only love, and Catherine of Siena describes Jesus as a fire always burning but never consuming. When Christians worship Jesus, they are sometimes encouraged by the worship leader to share descriptions of Jesus. Think about descriptions that you would share. You might like to write down some of your own descriptions, or ask members of a local church to write their short descriptions of Jesus.
Arrange the written descriptions on the cloth among the pictures of Jesus. Gather together some objects that might help to illustrate the descriptions of Jesus—for example, a loaf of bread, a toy sheep, a candle. Arrange these objects next to the appropriate description.

Stilling

Look at yourself in the mirror. Think about the person you are.

- Are you a son or a daughter…?
- Are you a brother or a sister…?
- Are you someone's friend…?

Think about what you like to do.

- Do you like sport…?
- Do you like to read…?

- Do you like to play computer games…?
- Do you enjoy sitting quietly…?

Think about God, your creator. Talk to God about yourself… the things you like about being you.

Talk to God about the things you might like to change.

- Do you get cross easily…?
- Would you like to be more helpful…?

Talk to God about the things you don't like about being you, things that you find hard to accept.

Ask God to help you see yourself as God sees you. Spend some time quietly thanking God for making you the person you are. Thank God for his love for you.

Bible focus

Then Jesus asked them, 'But who do you say I am?' Simon Peter spoke up, 'You are the Messiah, the Son of the living God.'
MATTHEW 16:15–16

Jesus was with the disciples and he wanted to know what people were saying about him. He listened to their answers and then asked the disciples, 'But who do you say I am?'

Staying with the story

Look at the pictures of Jesus. Are you surprised by some of the pictures?

Think about which picture you like best…

Think about which picture you like least…

Read some of the descriptions of Jesus...

Think about what they say to you about Jesus...

Think about whether or not you agree with them all...

Think about whether you like some descriptions better than others...

If Jesus asked you, 'Who do you say I am?' what would you reply?

Living with the story

Take a large sheet of paper and write Jesus' name on it in big letters. You could decorate the letters with crayons or colouring pens, or you may like to decorate them by sticking on coloured paper, fabric scraps or wool.

On the paper around Jesus' name, you could write or draw your descriptions or names for Jesus.

You may like to try writing a poem about Jesus and sticking it next to his name.

Prayer response

Lord Jesus, thank you for being everything I need. Please help me to understand more about who you are. Amen

Living the journey

Try one or more of the following activities.

■ Find out some more about Jesus. You could read some stories from the Gospels, or borrow a book, video or DVD from the library.

- Spend some more time talking with God about the person you are.
- Tell a friend what Jesus means to you.

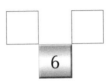

6

Saying thank you

Although this quiet corner can be used throughout the year, it is particularly appropriate for harvest time, the yellow base fabric being reminiscent of fields of ripening corn. We begin by looking at assorted tins and packets of food. By reading the labels, we can find the food's place of origin and match the food with the country of origin on a map of the world. Understanding where our food comes from and thinking about all the people involved in growing, producing and transporting it can help us to be more appreciative. We can then express our gratitude to God through thanksgiving.

The Bible focus turns our attention to spiritual food as we reflect on Jesus' words to the devil when he was tempted in the desert after his baptism. As we stay with the story, we think about Jesus as the bread that gives life (John 6:35). We taste bread and drink water as we reflect on Jesus' words and try to understand what he meant by them. As we grow spiritually, we may find that we become more thankful, turning more often towards God with gratitude.

Getting started

Arrange some yellow fabric on the floor or table top.

Place a large map of the world on the floor or table top.

Collect an assortment of food packets and tins, and arrange them on one side of the map of the world.

Place a jug of water and some small drinking glasses on a tray.

Place the tray on the opposite side of the map of the world from the food packets and tins.

Arrange some bread rolls or slices of bread on a plate. Place the plate on the tray alongside the jug of water and drinking glasses. (NB: If anyone using the quiet corner has a wheat allergy, make available some gluten-free bread from a local health food shop or supermarket.)

Place a book of graces next to the tray. It could be a book that you have bought, or you could make your own book of graces. Alternatively, you could ask your local school or children at church to tell you their favourite graces.

Alongside the basic craft box, have available some card circles or plain paper plates and some magazines containing pictures of food.

Stilling

Spend some time quietly looking at the food packets and tins.

Think about foods you like…

Think about foods you don't like…

Think about foods that are good for you…

Think about foods that are not good for you…

Think about the huge variety of food that is available…

Think about what it might feel like to be really hungry…

Look at the labels and find out what countries the foods come from.

Look at the world map. Can you match the packets and tins of food to the countries they come from?

Think about how many people were involved in growing, preparing, packaging, transporting and selling these packets and tins…

Spend some time quietly saying 'thank you' to God for all the people who help to provide you with food. You may like to say one or two of the prayers from the book of graces.

Bible focus

Jesus answered, 'The Scriptures say: "No one can live only on food. People need every word that God has spoken."'
MATTHEW 4:4

Food helps our bodies to grow strong and we need food to give us energy. Jesus tells us that we also need a different sort of food—to feed our souls as well as our bodies. We need spiritual food to help us grow strong in spirit and we need spiritual food to give us energy to do what God wants us to do. Jesus said, 'People need every word that God has spoken' (Matthew 4:4). The Bible is God's word and when we read the Bible we feed our souls.

Staying with the story

Jesus replied, 'I am the bread that gives life! No one who comes to me will ever be hungry. No one who has faith in me will ever be thirsty.'
JOHN 6:35

Jesus told them, '… My Father is the one who gives you the true bread from heaven. And the bread that God gives is the one who came down from heaven to give life to the world.'
JOHN 6:32B–33

Take a piece of bread in one hand and a glass of water in the other as you think about the words that Jesus spoke. As you taste the bread and drink the water, think about Jesus feeding your soul.

Spend some time quietly thanking Jesus for all the things that help to feed our souls, for all the things that help to make us happy and strong in spirit—our family… our friends…people in school or at church… God's words in the Bible.

Living with the story

Take a paper plate or circle of cardboard and write a 'thank you' prayer in the middle of it. Decorate the outside of the circle or the rim of the plate with pictures of food. You may enjoy drawing your own pictures or you may prefer to cut out and stick on some pictures from magazines.

You may like to fasten a loop of wool or string at the top to hang up your paper plate grace, or you may like to fasten the plate on the kitchen wall with sticky tack to remind you to say 'thank you' before eating food.

Prayer response

Loving God, thank you for all the good things in my life. Please help me always to be grateful for them. Amen

Living the journey

Try one or more of the following activities.

- Make a cube out of cardboard and write a different 'thank you' prayer on each face of the cube. Use the cube to help you say a 'thank you' prayer before eating food. (See page 106 for a cube net template that you can photocopy on to card.)
- Keep a collection box for one of the charities that helps hungry people. Whenever you buy sweets, put 10p in the box.
- Make your own book of graces. Ask your family and friends to tell you their favourite graces. Write them in a book and decorate the pages.

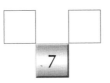

Creation

In this quiet corner we begin by thinking about the natural world. There is an opportunity to look at pictures and feel textures and shapes, which can help to create a sense of awe and wonder at the beauty and variety in the natural world. As our attention turns to our creator God, this sense of awe and wonder can lead into an expression of thanks and praise for all that God has given us.

The Bible focus leads us into a simplified story of creation, with opportunity to explore it in more detail if wished. As we think about God as creator and the pleasure he derived from creating the world, we begin to identify with his pleasure by thinking about our own creations. Our disappointment when something we have made is damaged can lead into concerns about environmental damage and what we can do to protect our planet.

Getting started

Arrange some blue fabric on the floor or table top.

Collect some artists' impressions of the creation of the world and display them on a wall behind the fabric.

Surround the creation images with pictures of space, mountain ranges, seascapes, rivers, plants, animals and people.

Scatter some leaves and pebbles among the pictures.

Place a simple version of the creation story among the pictures, together with a copy of the Bible opened at Genesis 1.

Place some clay or playdough on a tray. Place the tray to one side of the pictures.

Stilling

Spend some time quietly looking at the pictures.

Look at all the different colours... shapes... and textures...

Look at the leaves and pebbles... the different shapes and colours... and feel the textures...

- Think about our world.
- Think about the wonderful assortment of plants and trees...
- Think about the amazing number of birds in all their different colours and sizes...
- Think about the incredible variety of animal life...
- Think about God, the creator of the world, and how amazing it is that God created such variety and beauty.

Choose one of the pictures, or a leaf or pebble, and hold it in your hand. Spend some time quietly thanking God for all the good things in the world.

Bible focus

In the beginning God created the heavens and the earth.
GENESIS 1:1

On the very first day, God commanded light to shine, so now there was not just darkness, there was light and dark. God looked at the light and saw it was good. That was the end of the first day.

On the second day, God separated the waters to make space for the sky. God saw that this was good, and that was the end of the second day.

On the third day, God commanded the water under the sky to come together in one place so that there would be dry ground. He commanded the dry ground to produce all kinds of plants, and that's what happened. God looked at what he had done and it was good. That was the end of the third day.

On the fourth day, God gave us a way to keep time and mark the seasons. He made a powerful light to rule the day and the moon and stars to rule the night. God looked at what he had done and it was good. That was the end of the fourth day.

On the fifth day, God commanded the sea to be full of living creatures, and birds to fly above the earth. God looked at what he had done and it was good. That was the end of the fifth day.

On the sixth day, God commanded the earth to give life to all kinds of animals and reptiles. God created human beings to be like himself. He created men and women and he blessed them. God looked at what he had done. All of it was very good. That was the end of the sixth day.

By the seventh day, God had finished his work. God blessed the seventh day and made it special because on that day he rested from his work.

If you want to, you can read more about how God created the world, in Genesis 1:1—2:4 at the beginning of the Bible.

Staying with the story

Read the story of God creating the world.
See how God has created order and purpose…
See how pleased God was with all he had done…
Think about something that you enjoyed making.

- Were you pleased with it…?
- Did you want to show it to someone…?
- Did you want to give it to someone…?

Think about how you would feel if it was spoilt in some way. Think about how God feels when we spoil the wonderful world that he has given us. Think about what can you do to help look after the world.

Living with the story

Take a piece of clay or playdough and mould it with your fingers. Press the clay and squeeze it into different shapes...

Think about how you can create different textures...

You may like to make something useful with the clay, like a vase or candle holder.

You may like to make something decorative, like an animal, a person or a tree.

You may like to roll the clay back into a ball and come back to it later.

Prayer response

Loving God, thank you for the wonder of space and the beauty of the world. Please help me to use the earth's resources wisely and for the good of all people. Amen

Living the journey

Try one or more of the following activities.

- Take a shopping bag when you go shopping so that you don't need to use a plastic bag.
- When you get a new item of clothing, say 'thank you' to God for all the people involved in making it.

- Organize a litter pick in your local community. Advertise what you are doing and get local organizations involved. Supply disposable gloves for the 'pickers' and black bin bags for the litter.

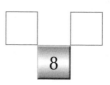

Praying for others

This quiet corner gives us an opportunity to think about the people who are important in our lives. Taking time in choosing pebbles to represent people offers space to think about individuals. People are continually being changed by circumstances, relationships with other people and by their relationship with God. At first glance, one pebble may look like any other pebble but, like people, each pebble is individually formed. The shape and texture of a pebble are the result of continual washing by the sea, which shapes and smoothes them. The careful arrangement of pebbles on a mat gives us the opportunity to think about our relationships. A pebble placed at a distance from the others may represent someone living far away or it may represent someone living in the same house but seemingly remote.

The Bible focus encourages us to pray continually. The trust and peace associated with prayer are explored through images of water and reassuring words from the Bible. In the same way that the pebble has been shaped from a rough piece of stone through continual washing and smoothing, so our lives are shaped by our continued relationship with others and with God. Taking a pebble to represent all our prayers, and putting it in the pebble pool full of water, symbolizes putting the people we love into God's hands and letting the Holy Spirit wash over them.

Getting started

Arrange some blue fabric on a table top to look like flowing water. Place a large bowl on the fabric on the table top. Ceramics or metal work well as there is a satisfying 'chink' when the pebble is placed in the water and makes contact with the bowl. However, for safety reasons, you may prefer to use a plastic bowl. Glass, although attractive, is not suitable for young children.

Half fill the bowl with water. Lay a fabric table mat (or a piece of brown felt) in front of the bowl. Arrange pictures of rivers, waterfalls and seascapes on the blue fabric surrounding the bowl of water. Include pictures of the sea or rivers washing over pebbles.

Next to the pictures arrange cards showing the words from the 'Staying with the story' section. Place a basket of pebbles next to the table mat.

Stilling

Look at the pebbles in the basket and choose a pebble to represent you... Look at the colours in your pebble and feel the texture... When you are ready, place the pebble on the mat...

Think about the people in your family... Look at the pebbles in the basket again and choose some more pebbles to represent members of your family... Arrange the pebbles on the mat, some near your pebble and maybe some far away...

Think about your friends... Look at the pebbles in the basket again and choose some more pebbles to represent your friends... Place the pebbles on the mat...

Think about others who are important to you... maybe your teacher or your pet... Choose some more pebbles to represent them and place the pebbles on the mat...

Look at all the pebbles on the mat... Spend some time quietly talking to God about all the people that the pebbles represent...

Bible focus

Never stop praying, especially for others. Always pray by the power of the Spirit. Stay alert and keep praying for God's people.
EPHESIANS 6:18

Staying with the story

God asks us to keep praying for others and he also asks us to trust him. Spend some time looking at the pictures of water as you read and think about the words on the cards.

I will bless those who trust me. They will be like trees growing beside a stream—trees with roots that reach down to the water, and with leaves that are always green. They bear fruit every year and are never worried by a lack of rain.
JEREMIAH 17:7–8

You, Lord, are my shepherd. I will never be in need. You let me rest in fields of green grass. You lead me to streams of peaceful water, and you refresh my life.
PSALM 23:1–3

I pray to you, God, because you will help me. Listen and answer my prayer!
PSALM 17:6

Gather all your pebbles together and put them back in the basket.

Choose one pebble to represent your prayers and hold it in your hand as you think about all the people who are important to you... Think about the pebble, the way it has been made, washed, shaped and smoothed by water... Think about God washing over and shaping the lives of the people you are praying for...

When you are ready, drop the pebble in the water and quietly thank God for listening and answering all your prayers.

Are there some other pebbles in the pool? Think about who put them there. You might not know who did it, but you can think about them all the same... Think about what situations and people the pebbles might represent... Pray for other people who have prayed at the pebble pool... You could use the following prayer.

Loving God, I bring to you all the people and situations that these pebbles represent. I pray also for all those who used these pebbles in their love and care for others. Amen

Living with the story

Make a pebble shape out of paper or card. You may like to write the words of Psalm 17:6 or Ephesians 6:18 on the pebble shape to remind you to pray. You may like to write the names of the important people in your life as a reminder to pray for them.

Prayer response

Lord Jesus, thank you for always being near to me. Please be near to all the people I love. Amen

Living the journey

Try one or more of the following activities.

- Keep a small pebble in your pocket or on your windowsill as a reminder to pray for others.

- Memorize the following words from Psalm 23:2–3 to remind you of God's love for you: 'You lead me to streams of peaceful water, and you refresh my life.'
- Make a special time each day to pray for the people who are important to you.

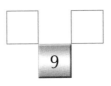

9

The journey

This quiet corner requires a lot of preparation, as you will need to make a finger labyrinth out of self-hardening clay well in advance. You will find further information in the chapter entitled 'The labyrinth' (see pages 27–34). However, you may wish to use the making of the labyrinth as an opportunity for a time of reflection in its own right. Ideas to help you do this are given alongside the full instructions for making the finger labyrinth.

In this quiet corner we begin by thinking generally about journeys and ways of travelling. Our thoughts are then guided to reflect on shorter, local journeys as we look at the map of our area. Time can be spent identifying places that we visit regularly and thinking of people we meet on our day-to-day travels. This can naturally turn into a time of thanksgiving to God.

The Bible focus turns our attention to a different sort of journey —a journey with Jesus, the shepherd who stands at the gate of the sheepfold. The finger labyrinth is used to explore the idea of going in and out of the sheepfold. Using fingers to walk while praying can give a sense of movement to prayer, as the labyrinth draws us towards the cross at the centre. If we use our non-dominant hand, this will slow down the journey. As our fingers move towards the centre, we can gain a real impression of being spiritually drawn into God's presence, protected under the shepherd's crook at the centre and strengthened as we return to the busyness of daily living.

As we explore the idea of journeying, we can gain a greater understanding of our own journey of faith with God.

Getting started

In advance, make a finger labyrinth out of self-hardening clay (see pages 32–34).

Arrange some brown fabric on the floor or table top. Place a map of your local area on the fabric. Gather together some pictures of modes of transport and arrange them around the edge of the map. Place a soft cushion on the fabric next to the map.

Place the finger labyrinth on the cushion.

Alongside the basic craft box, make available some blank postcards or postcard-sized card.

Stilling

Spend some time quietly looking at the pictures. Think about some journeys you have made.

- Where did you go…?
- Why did you go there…?
- How did you travel…?

Look at the map of your local area.

- Find the place where you live…
- Find places you have visited…
- Find your school, or the local school in your area…
- Find your doctor or dentist…
- Find your local park or playground…

Draw with your finger on the map to show the journeys you have made… As you draw with your finger, spend some time quietly thanking God for a journey you have made, the people you have met, the sights you have seen…

Bible focus

Jesus said, 'I am the gate. All who come in through me will be saved. Through me they will come and go and find pasture.'
JOHN 10:9

Jesus is like the shepherd who stands at the gate of his sheepfold. When the sheep are in the sheepfold, the shepherd closes the gate so that the sheep will be safe from wolves or foxes. When it is safe, the shepherd opens the gate and leads his sheep to pasture. The shepherd watches over his sheep while they eat.

Staying with the story

Use the finger labyrinth to explore 'coming and going through the gate'.

Sit on a chair or on the floor with the cushion comfortably on your lap. Make sure the labyrinth sits securely on the cushion.

Pause before touching the labyrinth and offer your journey to God...

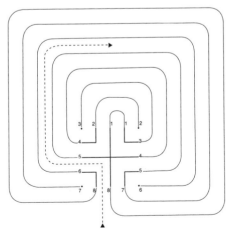

Close your eyes. Carefully feel for the entrance to the labyrinth and slowly move your finger along the path... If you are right-handed, use the middle finger of your left hand. If you are left-handed, use the middle finger of your right hand.

As you move towards the centre of the labyrinth, you could use the inward journey as a time of saying 'sorry' to God...

Take time to notice the curves of the path...

Think about how you feel when you think you're getting close to the middle...

Think about how you feel when the path seems to take you away from the centre...

Think about how you feel when you reach the centre...

Spend some time at the centre relaxing and enjoying time being with God...

When you are ready, start the journey away from the centre. You could use the outward journey as a time of asking God for help. You could ask God to strengthen you and help you at home, in school or at church.

As you reach the exit of the labyrinth, pause for a moment and give thanks to God for your journey.

Living with the story

Sometimes, when we go on holiday, we send postcards to our family or friends. Make a picture postcard showing what happened during your journey in and out of the labyrinth... You could draw a picture or write some words to remind you of how you felt, or if you thought God was speaking to you about something particular. Put the date on it and keep it in a safe place to remind you of your walk with God.

Prayer response

Lord Jesus, thank you for showing me the way to being still and quiet. As I become busy again, please help me make more times of being still and quiet with you. Amen

Living the journey

Try one or more of the following activities.

- Find out about people in the Bible who went on a journey. For example:
  - Mary and Joseph travelled from Nazareth to Bethlehem (Luke 2:3–5).
  - The apostle Paul travelled around the Mediterranean Sea so that he could tell people about Jesus (Acts 9—28).
  - Jesus made lots of journeys around the area of Galilee, and he eventually journeyed to Jerusalem (Luke 9:51).
  - Abraham journeyed from his home to the land of Canaan in response to God's call (Genesis 12:1).
  - Moses led the people of Israel away from Egypt and towards the promised land (Exodus 13:17–22).
  - Jonah travelled away from God and eventually, after being swallowed by a great big fish and spat out on a beach, to Nineveh to tell the people there about God (Jonah 1—4).

- As you read the stories, think about why people were making the journey and what they were learning about God as they travelled.
- The next time you travel somewhere, use some part of the journey quietly talking with God.

10

Running the race

This quiet corner is particularly appropriate during the lead-up to major sporting events such as the Olympic Games, athletics championships, the London Marathon, local sporting events or school sports days. We begin by looking at pictures of athletes, some well-known, others not. All have trained hard and worked to the best of their ability. Some are successful but others are disappointed.

As we think about the great achievements of athletes, whether they win or not, our thoughts turn to ourselves and something that we have strived to achieve, such as acquiring a new skill. Children may remember their frustration and subsequent sense of achievement over tasks such as learning to tie shoelaces or ride a bike. Older teenagers may be learning to drive a car. Adults may have fresh challenges as they start a new job. Learning is lifelong. As we reflect on our own achievements, we can be amazed at the power and complexity of human life and turn in gratitude to God our creator.

The Bible focus brings a spiritual dimension to achievement and strength as we begin to think about the gift of eternal life. As we read the words from 1 Corinthians 9:24–25, we are reminded that our ultimate goal is to follow Jesus and gain the crown of eternal life. Recognizing our reliance on Jesus and wanting to share his love, we are then encouraged to acknowledge the achievements and quiet perseverance of someone we know.

Getting started

Arrange some vibrantly coloured fabric on the floor or table top. You could choose the colours of your local running or football club, the Olympic colours, or colours that you associate with sporting achievements, such as the colours of the Wimbledon championships.

Place a trophy, medals, rosettes or other symbols of sporting achievement in the centre of the cloth.

Gather together pictures of athletes, including wheelchair athletes. Try to find pictures of local athletes of all ages as well as better-known international athletes. Try to include different responses as athletes react to their performances—defeat as well as victory, disappointment as well as the smiles of success. Arrange these pictures on the fabric.

Alongside the basic craft box items, you will need crêpe paper, shiny paper and ribbon.

Stilling

Spend some time quietly looking at the pictures of athletes.

Look at the expressions on their faces. Are they…

- pleased?
- disappointed?
- exhausted?
- full of energy?
- happy?

Think about something you have done that you have had to work really hard to achieve. It may be something small like learning to spell a long word, or it may be something bigger like learning to ride a bike. How did you feel when you achieved your goal?

Spend some time thanking God for making you such a special person, for helping you to meet new challenges and learn new skills.

Bible focus

Such a large crowd of witnesses is all around us! So we must get rid of everything that slows us down, especially the sin that just won't let go. And we must be determined to run the race that is ahead of us. We must keep our eyes on Jesus, who leads us and makes our faith complete.

HEBREWS 12:1–2A

You know that many runners enter a race, and only one of them wins the prize. So run to win! Athletes work hard to win a crown that cannot last, but we do it for a crown that will last for ever.

1 CORINTHIANS 9:24–25

But those who trust the Lord will find new strength. They will be strong like eagles soaring upward on wings; they will walk and run without getting tired.

ISAIAH 40:31

I have fought well. I have finished the race, and I have been faithful.

2 TIMOTHY 4:7

Staying with the story

Spend some time thinking about what it means to keep our eyes on Jesus.

What do you need to help you to follow Jesus…?

What is the crown that lasts for ever…?

What new strength do you need to ask God for…?

Eric Liddell was one of the 1924 Olympic Games competitors whose story is told in the film *Chariots of Fire*. He believed that God had called him to work as a missionary in China, but he said, 'God also made me fast, and when I run, I feel his pleasure. To win is to honour God.' He won his Olympic gold medal and then went to China. He remained focused on what God wanted him to do. As he served God by telling the people of China about Jesus, he continued to work for the crown that will last for ever.

What work is God calling you to do…?

What can you do to remain focused on what God wants you to do…?

What do you need to get rid of, that is slowing you down…?

Living with the story

Think about someone who you think deserves a medal. It could be someone who has done something special or it could be someone who quietly works hard all the time. Make a rosette for that person out of card and crêpe paper, or you may prefer to make a medal out of card, shiny paper and ribbon.

Prayer response

Loving God, thank you for making it possible for me to follow Jesus. Please help me to work for you and to serve you to the best of my ability. Amen

Living the journey

Try one or more of the following activities.

- Find some small achievement to celebrate every day.
- Praise someone for his or her achievements.
- Make a simple board game to help you think about following Jesus. Draw a race track on a piece of cardboard. Mark the start

and finish and divide the route into squares. Write instructions on the squares—for example, 'You got cross with the cat, go back 2 squares'; 'You helped wash the dishes, go on 3 squares.'

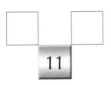

Jesus is... the good shepherd

Nowadays, children may have a limited understanding of the role of the shepherd, whether in New Testament times or the current day. Yet it is an important image for Christians, as the theme of the shepherd runs through the Bible from beginning to end. In this quiet corner we begin by thinking about pets and their care before turning our attention to the specific theme of sheep and shepherds. Most children have a pet or know someone who has one. We are encouraged to think about how we care for a pet, including providing a safe environment, food and water. As we think about the way we look after our pets, our thoughts turn towards God and his care for us. This can lead into a time of thanksgiving and acknowledgment of God's love for us.

The Bible focus reinforces the idea of care and protection by turning our attention to Jesus as the good shepherd who knows his sheep and whose sheep know him. Further ideas can be introduced from this passage in John's Gospel if we contrast the role of the shepherd and the hired worker. The idea of Jesus having other sheep that are not in the sheepfold could also be pursued. As we stay with the story, we use images and objects to help us reflect on the words of Psalm 23. Spending time thinking about the role of Jesus as a shepherd helps us to appreciate his love for us more fully.

Getting started

Arrange some green fabric on the floor or table top. Collect some pictures and models of pet animals. You could include some small soft toys. Arrange them to one side of the green cloth. Gather the following items together in a basket.

■ Some blue fabric to represent water
■ Some green fabric to represent pasture
■ Some brown fabric for pathways
■ Some dark grey fabric to create valleys
■ Some large rocks and stones

Place the basket to one side of the green cloth. Cut out some sheep shapes from card and place them in a small basket together with some pencils and coloured pencils. Place the basket on the green cloth.

Place a figure of Jesus in the centre of the cloth. See page 103 for details of where to obtain a wooden figure of Jesus. Alternatively, you may wish to trace the template on page 108 on to plywood, cut out with a jig saw and then smooth and wax to finish the model. (NB: Children may be able to help trace the outline on to plywood, and to smooth and wax the wood, but the figure will need to be cut out by an adult.) Place a copy of Psalm 23 next to the figure of Jesus.

Stilling

Spend some time looking at the pet animal pictures and soft toys.

Do you have a pet or do you know someone who has a pet...?

Choose the picture or soft toy you like best.

Think about the animal, bird or fish you have chosen. Think about what you would do if it was your pet.

• Where would you keep it...?
• What would you give it to eat and drink...?
• Does it need exercise...?

Think about all the care you would need to give your pet.

Think about all the care that God gives you. Spend some time quietly thanking God for all the love and concern he has for you.

Bible focus

Jesus said: 'I am the good shepherd. I know my sheep, and they know me.'
JOHN 10:14

Jesus says that he is the good shepherd who gives up his life for his sheep. He is not like a hired worker. A hired worker doesn't care for the sheep and runs away if there is any danger. The good shepherd doesn't run away. He stays with his sheep.

Jesus also says that he has other sheep that are not in the sheepfold. When they hear his voice, he must bring them together so that there will be one flock of sheep and one shepherd.

If Jesus is the shepherd, then who are the sheep?

Staying with the story

Read the words of Psalm 23:

You, Lord, are my shepherd.
I will never be in need.
You let me rest in fields of green grass.
You lead me to streams
of peaceful water,
and you refresh my life.

You are true to your name,
and you lead me
along the right paths.

I may walk through valleys
as dark as death,
but I won't be afraid.
You are with me,
and your shepherd's rod
makes me feel safe.

You treat me to a feast,
while my enemies watch.
You honour me as your guest,
and you fill my cup until it overflows.

Your kindness and love
will always be with me
each day of my life,
and I will live for ever
in your house, Lord.

Think about these words as you use the stones and pieces of material to create a country landscape. What colour material will you use to create safe paths... dark valleys... peaceful streams...?

Living with the story

Take a card sheep shape and write your name on it.

Move your sheep to different places in your country landscape.

Think about times when everything seems straightforward and easy, as you move your sheep on the safe pathway.

Think about times when life seems difficult, as you move your sheep over rough stones or through dark valleys.

As you think about peaceful places and hard places, move the figure of Jesus next to your sheep and feel the strength of his presence alongside you.

Prayer response

Lord Jesus, thank you that you know me and take care of me in bad times and good times. Amen

Living the journey

Try one or more of the following activities.

- Visit a farm and find out more about what the work of a shepherd involves.
- A Christian minister is often referred to as the 'shepherd' of his or her flock. Ask your local minister what it means to be a shepherd in the church.
- Learn the words of Psalm 23 to help you remember that Jesus is always alongside you.

12

The armour of God

In this quiet corner we begin by thinking about protective clothing. We are encouraged to think about what we need protection against. Protective clothing is worn by people in numerous occupations and for various leisure pursuits. Dentists and medical staff wear masks and aprons or overalls to safeguard themselves against germs. Builders and decorators may wear boiler suits, dust masks and safety helmets. Road workers wear fluorescent jackets so that they can be seen clearly. Police officers and soldiers may wear protective body armour. As we think about all the ways in which we protect ourselves, this can lead into a time of being thankful to God for all the things and all the people that help to keep us safe.

The Bible focus helps to turn our attention to the need to protect ourselves spiritually. We think about God as our protector as we consider some images in the Bible, and we think about God as the provider who gives us all the strength we need to protect us from temptation.

Getting started

Arrange some red fabric on the floor or table top.

Collect some pictures of people wearing protective clothing for various leisure activities, such as cycling, mountaineering or skateboarding, and for work, such as dentist, builder, firefighter, soldier, cook or cleaner. Arrange the pictures on the cloth.

Gather together one or two examples of protective clothing, such as a safety helmet, a pair of goggles or some earmuffs, and place them amongst the pictures.

Collect some pictures relating to the Bible focus, such as a high rock or mountain, a castle, a shield, a cave and a bird with young (preferably an eagle). Place them in a basket to one side of the cloth.

Stilling

Spend some time quietly looking at the people in the photographs.

Look at the special protective clothing they are wearing.

Think about what these people need to be protected from...

Think about what would happen if these people didn't wear protective clothing...

Think about what special clothes you wear sometimes to keep you safe...

Think about all the times when you feel safe and protected...

When you are ready, spend some time talking to God, thanking him for all the things that help to keep you safe and for all the people who help to keep you safe.

Bible focus

Keep us from being tempted and protect us from evil.
MATTHEW 6:13

We need to protect our souls from harm in the same way that we protect our bodies from injury. The good news is that God is our protector but, just as people need to make the choice to wear protective clothing to keep them safe, so too we need to make the choice to obey God in order for him to protect our souls from harm.

Staying with the story

As you read the following words, think about the different ways in which God is described as our protector. You may like to look at some of the pictures in the basket.

Our Lord and our God, you are my mighty rock, my fortress, my protector. You are the rock where I am safe. You are my shield, my powerful weapon, and my place of shelter.
2 SAMUEL 22:2–3

The Lord was like an eagle teaching its young to fly, always ready to swoop down and catch them on its back.
DEUTERONOMY 32:11

Hide me in the shadow of your wings.
PSALM 17:8B

Think about which image helps you feel safe and protected...
 Think of another image of God as your protector...
 You might like to draw a place where you feel safe and protected.
 You may like to read these words from a hymn about God's protection, which was written by Cecil F. Alexander in 1889. The lyrics to the hymn are translated from a Gaelic poem called 'St Patrick's Lorica' (lorica means 'breastplate'), which are said to have been composed by St Patrick. You could say the words as a prayer.

Christ be with me, Christ within me,
Christ behind me, Christ before me,
Christ beside me, Christ to win me,
Christ to comfort and restore me,
Christ beneath me, Christ above me,
Christ in quiet, Christ in danger,
Christ in hearts of all that love me,
Christ in mouth of friend and stranger.

God protects us in another way. God gives us all we need to be strong to protect ourselves from temptation to do wrong.

Let the mighty strength of the Lord make you strong... Be ready! Let the truth be like a belt around your waist, and let God's justice protect you like armour. Your desire to tell the good news about peace should be like shoes on your feet. Let your faith be like a shield, and you will be able to stop all the flaming arrows of the evil one. Let God's saving power be like a helmet, and for a sword use God's message that comes from the Spirit.
EPHESIANS 6:10 AND 14–17

Living with the story

Imagine you are clothing yourself in the armour of God...

Fasten the belt of truth around your waist. This reminds you to be always truthful and to seek the truth.

Put on the body armour or jacket of justice. Try always to be fair and to treat other people as you would like them to treat you.

Put on your shoes so that you are ready to go and spread the good news of Jesus to your friends.

Hold your faith on your arm like a shield. Trust God at all times and in all places.

Put on the helmet of God's saving power. This helmet comes with a radio link so that you can speak with God and God can speak with you.

The word of God is your sword of protection. Try to get to know your Bible by reading a little each day.

Prayer response

Loving God, thank you that you are my protector. Please help me to stay true to you and to let your strength make me strong. Amen

Living the journey

Try one or more of the following activities.

- Every morning when you get dressed, imagine that you are putting on the whole armour of God and remind yourself about God's protection for you.
- Spend a little time each day reading the Bible. One of the Gospels, especially Mark's or Luke's, is a good place to start.
- When you see someone wearing protective clothing, say a quick prayer for that person and thank God for his protection.

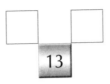

Circling prayer

In this quiet corner we are exploring the idea of circling, which is one of the major features of Celtic prayer. We begin by looking at round objects and develop the idea of things being surrounded and contained within circles. As we move on to consider the circle as a symbol of God's eternal care, we can move into a time of quiet thankfulness to God for his care and provision for us.

Our Bible focus reinforces this understanding of God's eternal care. We are then encouraged to move into a practical exploration of encircling prayer as we relate it to ourselves. This could be extended to include prayer for others.

Getting started

Arrange some green fabric on the floor or table top. Collect some small objects that have a circular shape, such as a bowl, a cup or a frisbee. Display these objects on the green cloth. Collect some pictures of objects that have a circular shape, such as a pond, a wheel, a tyre, a flowerbed or a castle. Arrange the pictures among the objects on the green cloth.

Write some 'feeling' words on separate pieces of card—for example, hope, fear, joy, sadness, peace, unrest, calm, hurt and so on. Try to balance the emotions so that there are the same number of positive feelings as negative. Place the cards in a basket to one side of the cloth. Place some blank cards in the basket with the words.

Stilling

Spend some time quietly looking at the pictures. Notice the shapes in the pictures. Touch the objects. Feel their roundness.

Think about what they are used for...

Think about which of them holds something inside...

Think about which of them keeps something outside...

Think about being cared for inside a circle.

Spend some time quietly thanking God for his eternal care and provision for you.

Bible focus

You are merciful, Lord! You are kind and patient and always loving. You are good to everyone, and you take care of all your creation.
PSALM 145:8–9

Staying with the story

Christians in the early Celtic church had a special way of understanding God's love and eternal provision. The Celtic word was *caim*, which was a protective circle. People imagined a circle drawn around themselves and the people they loved. Sometimes they would actually draw a circle around themselves by making a mark on the ground with a stick. Sometimes they would draw an imaginary circle around themselves with their pointed finger. Their prayer was 'Circle me, O God.' They believed that God was close to them and not far away.

Try drawing an imaginary circle around yourself...

You might like to think about the following words as you imagine yourself in the circle of God's love.

You, Lord, never fail to have pity on me; your love and faithfulness always keep me secure.
PSALM 40:11

The Lord loves justice, and he won't ever desert his faithful people. He always protects them.
PSALM 37:28

The Lord is your protector, there at your right side to shade you from the sun... The Lord will protect you now and always wherever you go.
PSALM 121:5 and 8

Living with the story

Draw a circle on a large sheet of paper. Draw a picture of yourself inside the circle. If the circle is large enough, you could stand inside the circle.

■ Think about what you would like to keep in the circle with you...
■ Think about what you would like to keep outside the circle...

Look at the words in the basket. You may like to put some of them inside your circle. You may like to put some outside your circle. You may like to write your own words or draw pictures on the blank cards.

As you arrange your words and pictures, you could say your own Celtic prayer, putting your own words in the spaces below.

Circle me, O God,
keep .... within,
keep .... out.

Prayer response

Loving God, thank you that you are so near to me. Please help me to feel your loving presence surrounding me, wherever I am and whatever I am doing. Amen

Living the journey

Try one or more of the following activities.

- Imagine God at your right side, giving you shade and protection, now and wherever you go.
- Use the circling prayer 'Circle me, O God...' as part of your daily prayers. You may find it helpful as you start the day, or you may prefer to use it at the end of the day as you settle down to sleep.
- Make a bracelet or wristband to remind you that God encircles you with his love and protection. You could make one out of a strip of leather or fabric or you could plait some embroidery thread or wool.

14

The Celtic knot

This quiet corner uses the idea of Celtic knotwork to help us think about God and eternity. The Celtic knot can be seen almost everywhere—on T-shirts, birthday cards, giftwrap, bookmarks, mugs and jewellery. It can also be seen on crosses in churchyards and in woodwork inside churches. The Celtic knot has no beginning and no end and symbolizes the eternal God. Like the knot, God is without beginning and without end.

Some knotwork designs also help us think about the Trinity— God the Father, God the Son and God the Holy Spirit. Even the simplest designs can help us understand the sense of community within the Trinity. The Father, Son and Holy Spirit have equal standing within the design and yet they are intertwined and supportive of one another.

It would be particularly appropriate to use the ideas in this quiet corner to celebrate the anniversary of one of the Celtic saints, such as Brigid (1 February) or David (1 March). If so, you may like to include a short history of the saint, together with the special prayer or Collect used in the Anglican Church. You could also display symbols associated with the saint. For example, for David you could display the Welsh flag, a leek or a daffodil. For Brigid you could provide materials and instructions to make a St Brigid's cross. See *A-cross the World* for the story of St Brigid (or Bridget) and instructions to make a woven cross like St Brigid's.

Getting started

Arrange some green fabric on the floor or table top. Collect some examples of Celtic design, such as a T-shirt, a piece of jewellery, bookmarks, giftwrap, or a Celtic cross. Arrange them on the green cloth.

Collect some pictures of Celtic design, such as wood carving in a church or illuminated letters, and some pictures of Celtic crosses. Arrange them on the green cloth.

Draw or photocopy some simple Celtic designs and place them on a tray with some coloured pencils and some plain paper. (See page 109 for a template to help you.)

Stilling

Spend some time quietly looking at the objects on the cloth.
Think about what they are used for...
Look at the designs on the objects and in the pictures.
Think about which one you like best...
Think about why you like this one best...
Hold one of the designs in your hand. Use your finger to trace the design.

- Where will you start...?
- Where will you finish...?

Notice the way the lines go over and under one another. Are there any loose ends?

Is there a beginning? Is there an end?

These patterns are designed to help us think about God. God is eternal and has no beginning or end. As you trace the design with your finger, spend some time quietly praising God and thanking God for always being there.

Bible focus

I pray that honour and glory will always be given to the only God, who lives for ever and is the invisible and eternal King! Amen.
1 TIMOTHY 1:17

Can you think of some words of praise that will give honour and glory to God?

Here are some words to think about while you move your finger over the patterns.

Our Lord, you are eternal! Your word will last as long as the heavens.
PSALM 119:89

You, Lord, are the only true and living God. You will rule for all time.
JEREMIAH 10:10A

Staying with the story

God is eternal and he gives us the promise of eternal life, too.

Eternal life is to know you, the only true God, and to know Jesus Christ, the one you sent.
JOHN 17:3

God loved the people of this world so much that he gave his only Son, so that everyone who has faith in him will have eternal life and never really die.
JOHN 3:16

Choose one of the designs on the tray and think about God's promise of eternal life while you colour in the pattern. You may prefer to draw your own pattern, weaving the lines in and out and under and over.

Living with the story

Look at the pictures of Celtic crosses. Take some card and try making your own Celtic cross out of cardboard. You could draw designs on your cross. You might like to glue pieces of string or wool on to your cross. Remember to weave them under and over each other and hide all the ends.

Prayer response

Loving God, your Son Jesus died so that we can have eternal life. Please help me always to remember your promise. Amen

Living the journey

Try one or more of the following activities.

- Visit your local churchyard and look at some of the inscriptions on the gravestones. Think about what they say to you about God's promise of eternal life.
- Learn one of the following verses from John's Gospel to help you remember God's promise to you.

Eternal life is to know you, the only true God, and to know Jesus Christ, the one you sent.
JOHN 17:3

God loved the people of this world so much that he gave his only Son, so that everyone who has faith in him will have eternal life and never really die.
JOHN 3:16

- Use a Celtic knot design to make a birthday card for someone.

Bible index

Bibliography

Bibles

The Global Bible for Children, Authentic, 2005
Contemporary English Version, HarperCollins, 1991
Good News Bible (2nd edition), The Bible Societies, 1994

Children's story Bibles

The Barnabas Children's Bible, Rhona Davies, Barnabas, 2007
The Barnabas Schools' Bible, Rhona Davies, Barnabas, 2007
My First Bible, Leena Lane, Barnabas, 2006

Books on reflection with children

Beyond the Candle Flame, Brian Ogden and Jo Dobbs, Barnabas, 2006
A-cross the World, Martyn Payne and Betty Pedley, Barnabas, 2004

Picture books

The Life of Jesus through the Eyes of an Artist, Paul Forsey, Barnabas, 2005

Books about labyrinths

Living the Labyrinth, Jill Kimberly Hartwell Geoffrion, The Pilgrim Press, 2000

Books on prayer

How to Pray, John Pritchard, SPCK, 2002
Dialogues with Silence, Thomas Merton, SPCK, 2002
The Edge of Glory, David Adam, SPCK, 1985
Sounds of Eternity, J. Philip Newell, The Canterbury Press, 2002

Song books

Junior Praise, Marshall Pickering, 1986
The Source, Kevin Mayhew, 1998

Artefacts

Wooden figures are available from:

St Michael's Cottage Crafts
Bowthorpe Community Trust
Bowthorpe Hall Road
Bowthorpe
Norwich
NR5 9AA
Telephone: 01603 746106
Email: bowthorpe.trust@tiscali.co.uk

Templates

Cube net

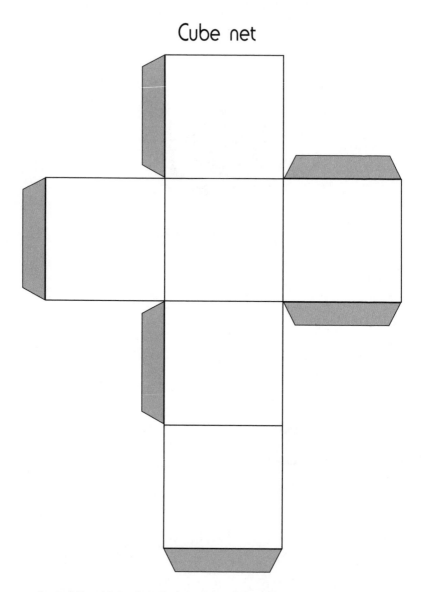

Labyrinth

Reproduced with permission from *Creative Ideas for Quiet Corners* published by BRF 2008 (978 1 84101 546 0)
www.barnabasinchurches.org.uk

Figure of Jesus

Celtic cross

Reproduced with permission from *Creative Ideas for Quiet Corners* published by BRF 2008 (978 1 84101 546 0)

www.barnabasinchurches.org.uk

Play and Pray through Lent

Ed. Kay Warrington

Play and Pray through Lent draws on the child's natural sense of playfulness and creativity to enable spiritual growth, by linking the world of the child with the great Lenten themes of the Church.

Based on the Revised Common Lectionary, the book suggests ways in which children can engage with the story of Easter during the six weeks of Lent in a creative way. This is achieved using simple visual items, such as a story cloth and card figures, along with 'talk about' ideas, Bible focus, prayers and Sunday worship suggestions.

ISBN 978 1 84101 392 3   £9.99

Play and Pray through Advent

Lynn Chambers, Kay Warrington and Nia Catrin Williams

Play and Pray through Advent encourages children and families to participate in the events surrounding the birth of Jesus, his early years and the beginning of his ministry.

In the same format as *Play and Pray through Lent*, the book suggests ways in which children can engage creatively with the story by exploring themes from the Gospels and preparing for the Sunday worship of their local church.

ISBN 978 1 84101 567 5   £9.99

Barnabas books are available from your local Christian bookshop or, in case of difficulty, direct from BRF using the order form below.

Resourcing people to work with 3–11s

in churches and schools

- Articles, features, ideas
- Training and events
- Books and resources
- www.barnabasinchurches.org.uk